GARDEN
STYLE

SELINA LAKE

GARDEN STYLE

Inspirational styling for your outside space

Photography by Rachel Whiting

RYLAND PETERS & SMALL
LONDON • NEW YORK

Senior designer Megan Smith
Senior commissioning editor Annabel Morgan
Location research Jess Walton
Head of production Patricia Harrington
Art director Leslie Harrington
Editorial director Julia Charles
Publisher Cindy Richards

First published in 2018 by
Ryland Peters & Small
20–21 Jockey's Fields
London WC1R 4BW
and
341 E 116th Street
New York, NY 10029

www.rylandpeters.com

10 9 8 7 6 5 4 3 2 1

ISBN 978-1-84975-925-0

A CIP record for this book is available from the British Library.

Library of Congress CIP data has been applied for.

Printed and bound in China

CONTENTS

EVERYTHING IN THE GARDEN'S LOVELY
Whether you are drawn to English country gardens (opposite above left) or cool Scandi city plots, in *Garden Style* I show how to make the most of any outdoor space. There's plenty of inspiration when it comes to creating relaxing spots where you can enjoy your own little patch of the great outdoors (left and opposite above right). I explore greenhouses, sheds and summerhouses (opposite below right) and take a closer look at bringing the garden indoors in the shape of home-grown flowers (opposite below left). You may even be inspired to grow your own veggies and eat them in a garden dining room all summer long!

INTRODUCTION

The happiest times of my life have been spent in the garden. As a little girl, my parents' garden was my and my sister Aimee's playground: we made dens in the greenhouse, created 'perfume' from mum's roses and followed dad around, helping him with his garden chores. When my husband and I bought our first house, we inherited a much-neglected plot and creating a garden out of it together has been a wonderful experience. But despite my ever-increasing love of plants and getting down to work in the borders, you won't be surprised to hear that it's styling the garden that I enjoy most. Making our little patch of green look good with plants, containers, lights and my collection of vintage 'gardenalia' makes me happy, and it extends our living space too.

In this book, I share tips on how to style different areas of the garden. including outdoor living spaces, alfresco dining rooms and even the humble garden shed. Look out for my styling tips and simple projects as well as details of my favourite plants so that you can grow them yourself. I hope the book will inspire you to make the most of any outside space, no matter what its size and shape, and to transform your own plot into a beautiful and relaxing leafy retreat.

GARDEN INSPIRATIONS

MY GARDEN MOODBOARD

My own garden style changes with the seasons, but I feel inspired by beautiful flowers all year round. I love visiting garden centres and plant shops, and browsing garden-related images via social media.

Wild Flowers of Europe

GARDENS I LOVE

The best places to seek out garden inspiration.

Walking through a beautiful garden on a sunny day is, for me, the perfect way to spend free time, and I always have my camera with me to take photos of plants, flowers and ideas that inspire me. I like looking at planting combinations, but it's the details I find most interesting. For example, take the structures that support plants - what are they made of, what style are they, do they suit the rest of the garden? If there's a chance to see behind the scenes where the magic happens, in the sheds or greenhouses, then I'm there.

There are so many amazing gardens worth visiting, some open to the public, some owned by neighbours and friends and some that you can only glimpse on TV. If an opportunity presents itself to view a garden you haven't seen, visit and have a good look round.

JARDIN DES TUILERIES

This is a public park laid out in a French formal garden style near the Louvre Museum in Paris, situated on the banks of the River Seine. Relax around the ponds on the famous green Luxembourg chairs by Fermob.

DAVID AUSTIN ROSE GARDENS

More than 700 different varieties of English roses, and possibly the best rose gardens in the world. Near Wolverhampton, UK, June is the best month to visit.

ERIKSDALSLUNDEN

A colony of private gardens in Stockholm, where each plot has a little cabin. You can't enter the gardens without permission, but you can walk along the paths that link the gardens and peer over the low fences and borders.

WINDSOR GREAT PARK

My parents used to take us here. It's a special place, covering more than 1,940 hectares/4,800 acres, and with Windsor Castle nearby I have even seen the Queen on a few occasions.

PERCH HILL

Garden designer, author, TV presenter and mail-order plant specialist Sarah Raven sometimes opens her fabulous and inspiring private garden in East Sussex, UK.

RHS WISLEY

The Royal Horticultural Society's garden at Wisley in the county of Surrey is one of four gardens run by the RHS (the others are Harlow Carr, Hyde Hall and Rosemoor). Luckily for me, Wisley is very close to our home.

GIVERNY

Artist Claude Monet's garden at Giverny, north-west of Paris, richly deserves its iconic status. It's really two gardens in one - a beautiful flower garden and a Japanese-inspired water garden, site of the mesmerizing waterlilies.

GREAT DIXTER GARDENS

Great Dixter, in East Sussex, was the family home of gardener and writer Christopher Lloyd. Now this historic house and garden have become a place of pilgrimage for horticulturists worldwide.

ROSENDALS TRÄDGÅRD

A Stockholm garden foundation with the purpose of widening public knowledge of biodynamic gardening and landscaping, with a rose garden, cut flower field, vegetable gardens, vineyard and impressive composting system.

MUM AND DAD'S GARDEN

Not a garden everyone can visit, but one I couldn't leave off the list! My parents' English garden is where I spent a happy childhood.

DAVID AUSTIN ROSES

In a corner of the David Austin rose garden, scented climbing and rambling pink and yellow English roses scramble over a wooden pergola leading to a white gate. The garden is well worth a visit, especially in June, when the sheer abundance of blooms is amazing!

FLOWER SHOWS & OPEN GARDENS

A lovely day out, full of garden ideas and buying opportunities.

My number one event of the year has to be the Royal Horticultural Society (RHS) Hampton Court Palace Flower Show. A day there involves marvelling at show gardens, buying plants from specialist suppliers and soaking up the atmosphere. The RHS is known for hosting fabulous events, including the world-famous Chelsea Flower Show in London, which I also love to visit. The photo below right is from the Hampton Court show, featuring an informal take on a classic border.

In 2017, one of my favourite garden designers, Dorthe Kvist of Melt Design Studio exhibited her Wild and Wonderful urban oasis garden at the Haveselskabet Cph Garden Show in Copenhagen. She demonstrated the latest trends in garden design while espousing sustainability, biodiversity, recycling and an ethos for growing your own food, and all in a small space aimed at showing city-dwellers how to make the most of a tiny plot (below left).

Another way to experience gardens at their best is by visiting them on open days. In the UK, the National Garden Scheme raises funds for charity, with garden owners opening their private gardens to the public and charging an entry fee that goes to the charity.

PUTTING ON A SHOW

Dorthe Kvist's Wild and Wonderful garden at the Haveselskabet Cph Garden Show in Copenhagen (below left) was all about 'cosiness, authenticity, relaxation and retreat,' while James Callicott's gravel garden 'By the Sea' was a favourite at the Hampton Court Palace Flower Show in 2017 (below right).

VISITING OPEN GARDENS

I always enjoy looking round other people's gardens, and in the UK the National Garden Scheme gives garden lovers an opportunity to visit interesting, beautiful and characterful private gardens. The entrance fees charged are donated to a variety of nursing charities. Over 3,700 gardens participate each year, raising more than £50 million to date.

Egenodlade
biodynamiska
PLANTOR
Rosendals Trädgård
GAMLA
LERKRUKOR
20:-

GARDEN CENTRES & NURSERIES

Where I can easily while away an entire weekend.

SHOPPING HEAVEN

This exquisitely styled garden display (opposite) is inside the greenhouse shop at Rosendals Trädgård in Sweden, one of the most magical garden shops I've visited and filled to the rafters with wonderful items to make your garden beautiful. For plant aficionados, specialist nurseries are places to discover different varieties and to see the plants before you buy. Neat flowerbeds of foxgloves, iris and sneezeweed (above left) and massed dahlias (above right) on show at two such nurseries.

Visiting garden centres, flower shops and plant specialists is essential if, like me, you enjoy botanical spaces where you can also shop. The best stores change their displays and stock regularly, meaning each time you visit there's something new and seasonal to inspire you.

My favourite garden shops are those that stock vintage gardenalia alongside an array of healthy plants and new finds. Burford Garden Company in Oxfordshire has become a favourite destination, as they stock lots of Scandinavian brands, items from smaller independent companies and antiques for the garden. Closer to home in Surrey are two lovely garden shops that my husband discovered while out cycling - Moutan Garden Shop, near Hook in Hampshire, which always has a good selection of galvanized planters, and Long Barn Lavender Growers near Winchester, which has a lovely café and, as you would expect, lots of varieties of lavender. In London, I often visit Scarlet & Violet, an inspiring flower shop owned by Vic Brotherson. Her flowers are beautiful and so is the interior of the shop, with vintage crate shelving peppered with antique vases, ceramic ornaments, botanical postcards and other collectibles.

Recently I had the pleasure of visiting Blomsterskuret flower shop in Copenhagen. The exterior of the small shop is painted black, which makes the colourful flowers pop out against the dark backdrop.

All these places and more enrich my gardening experience, as I love seeing how other creative people style and display garden-related items, and I always leave feeling inspired to try something new.

There are garden centres you go to for compost/soil and gravel, and others where you can delight in styled garden settings, gorgeous cafés and covetable gardenalia. These include Zetas Trädgård and Rosendals Trädgård in Stockholm, Löddeköpinge Plantskola, near Malmö, Petersham Nurseries in Richmond (right and below) and Burford Garden Company in Oxfordshire (bottom). On my wish list to visit are New York's Urban Garden Center and Terrain, which has four stores across the USA. If you visit somewhere that inspires you, take note of how they do things – visiting Stockholm's Zetas Trädgård (below right and opposite) provided me with lots of new ideas.

1

MY TOP TEN EASY-TO-GROW GARDEN PLANTS

I found it so difficult to whittle this list down to just ten entries, but here are the plants I recommend. Of course, as my knowledge grows, this list is likely to change, but that is just one of the many joys of gardening.

1. SWEET PEAS

Lathyrus odoratus

I think sweet peas are among the most rewarding flowers to grow. Select the best seeds you can and choose a variety renowned for its fragrance. I grow these every year and I'm always amazed by how many flowers they produce. The more you pick, the more you get, so don't hold back from snipping off the blooms.

2. GERANIUMS

Geranium

I opt for the perennial varieties, as they return each year and produce more blooms each season. Every geranium in our garden is a different shade of pink and they are a good border filler, flowering from spring through to late summer.

3

4

3. FOXGLOVES

Digitalis purpurea

Our garden just wouldn't be complete without its mass of foxgloves. They are my go-to plant and I love the way they self-seed everywhere, surprising us with new plants each year. I always buy white and apricot varieties to mix in with the common pink foxglove.

4. HOLLYHOCKS

Alcea rosea

A tall, dramatic plant with open trumpet-shaped flowers, these fit in perfectly with our cottage garden planting scheme. They need to be planted in full sun in moist, rich, well-drained soil and watered regularly, as they are thirsty. They also self-seed, which is an added bonus.

5

6

7

10

5. TULIPS

Tulipa

Tulip bulbs are a great addition to the garden, as you sometimes forget where you planted them and they pop up in spring with minimal care and attention. This autumn I've planted the pink and white Danceline variety on Monty Don's advice - I can't wait to see them bloom.

6. CLEMATIS

Clematis

Also known as old man's beard, clematis is one of the most popular garden plants and no wonder; this versatile plant can be grown on walls, pergolas, frames, in containers or left to scramble just about anywhere.

8

9

7. ALLIUMS

Allium

From the same plant family as onions and chives, alliums grow from bulbs and produce tall stems with a pompom flower head. Super easy to grow, simply plant the bulbs 15–20 cm/6–8 inches deep in autumn and wait until spring to see them bloom.

8. ROSES

Rosa

With so many roses to choose from, you can grow them in pots, beds and borders, climbing up walls or fences, or use them to create living structures such as arches. They have the most amazing scents, which I wish I could bottle and wear every day as perfume.

9. JASMINE

Jasminum

Jasmines grow well in moist, well-drained soil, and have a delicious scent and pretty flowers. They also make great conservatory or greenhouse plants. There are many different varieties to choose from, so have a good look around your plant centre or specialist nursery.

10. NARCISSI

Narcissus

These delicate spring bulbs are my mum's favourite flowers, so whenever I see them, I think of her. My top picks would be *Narcissus* 'Thalia', a classic ivory Victorian variety, and 'Sweet Smiles', because it has a lovely scent and matures to a dainty shell-pink hue.

FLEURS

PRINTS, PATTERNS & PAPER

Taking inspiration from botanical drawings and paintings.

I often find that a botanical drawing, painting or print will inspire an idea for my garden. You may be drawn to colour combinations or patterns you can replicate in your planting schemes. Or perhaps you want to adopt a botanical look in your outdoor rooms by introducing patterns and prints in the form of printed textiles for cushions, awnings, sun umbrellas or napkins.

Vintage botanical prints are having an 'on trend' moment - search for genuine ones at fairs and flea markets or look online for modern wall charts drawn in a vintage style. I like making my own black-and-white prints, and use small decorative brass bulldog clips from Anthropologie to display them on an internal wall.

There are so many talented artists and designers - current and historic - who have been inspired by flowers and gardens, interpreting the natural world in a variety of styles and media. I particularly like the work of Nadia Nörbom, who has produced prints of her delicate, detailed botanical paintings for Rosendals Trädgård garden shop in Stockholm as well as illustrations for a book on wild edible plants.

BOTANICAL BY DESIGN

A vintage Swedish botanical wall chart (opposite) is completely at home surrounded by plants and industrial pipes in the garden centre at Rosendals Trädgård in Stockholm, Sweden. Delicate work by Nadia Nörbom (above) looks sweet clipped to a wire display line above a bed of nasturtiums. Displayed indoors, both artworks bring the outside in, and perhaps they will inspire you to plant new flowers and plants based on those depicted in the prints.

PRETTY PAGES & SEED PACKETS

I have a passion for collecting vintage botanical books. I adore and admire the intricate detail of the illustrations and I use any loose pages to decorate the interior walls and windows of my garden shed (left and above left). I also struggle to throw away empty seed packets, especially those with pretty packaging (above). I need to come up with a craft project to reuse them in a decorative way, but for now they are carefully stored in an old wooden seed tray (opposite), waiting for inspiration to strike!

BARR'S SEEDS
FOR FLOWER & KITCHEN GARDEN
OF FINEST SELECTED STRAINS & TESTED GROWTH

FINDING FLORAL INSPIRATION

A garden-room writing desk (above) has been styled with cosmos and mallow blooms with recycled glass bottles serving as vases, while my DIY botanical wall prints adorn the rough wood-clad walls, blending the cosy space with the garden beyond. The striking flower-patterned wallpaper decorating this Swedish wooden cabin (opposite) is Alicia 6701 from Beautiful Traditions collection by BoråsTapeter. I've arranged branches of beautifully fragrant fresh mock orange blossom in a galvanized bucket to continue the floral theme, echoing the sweeping lines of the wallpaper behind. Cushion covers in a bold botanical print by Abigail Borg (right) are perfect for a garden room, drawing inspiration from the natural world outside.

SOCKERBOLAGET

DECORATING YOUR GARDEN

POTS & CONTAINERS

Ring the changes with different sizes, shapes and finishes.

PATINATED POTS

This old zinc bucket makes a great home for a pink mophead hydrangea surrounded by lush green leaves (above left). Zetas Trädgård in Stockholm stocks a fabulous collection of clay pots, many of them with a beautiful, gently aged appearance (above centre). An old metal urn planted with jade plant (*Crassula ovata*) adds intriguing detail to a sunny garden room (above right). A pleasing array of old, new and reclaimed containers in Danish garden designer Dorthe Kvist's garden (opposite).

Pots and containers are one of the most easy and inexpensive ways to jazz up any outside space. Pretty much any vessel can work as a planter, but it needs to be the right size, shape and material for the plant you want it to hold. Drainage is important if roots aren't to become waterlogged, so if your chosen container doesn't have holes in the base, you'll need to drill some. Also think about weight – a large planter filled with soil can be almost impossible to move, so make sure you're happy with a pot's position before you fill it with compost and plant it up. If you plan on moving planters, one solution is to screw casters to the base of wooden containers so you can push them around your deck or terrace.

What I'm most interested in is, of course, the style of the container, and how it works with plant colours and textures and the rest of the garden. I'm always inspired by the many Scandinavian gardens I have visited, which tend to feature fairly classic designs with a nod to salvaged and vintage gardenalia. To get this relaxed Scandi look, mix galvanized metal vessels with planted-up wooden crates and chunky black or grey clay pots.

I'm not a huge fan of bold or colourful containers, as I think plants and flowers themselves are best at contributing a colourful element, but if you're looking for something unusual, consider adapting old metal washtubs or animal drinking troughs that once lived on farms.

STYLE TIP

For me, a potting shed is a creative space that should be both beautiful and practical. In my own shed (opposite), I keep everything out on display – everything, that is, except unsightly, garish plastic pots and tools, which are hidden out of sight. The pine shelf unit was left in our house by the previous owner, and I use it to display an array of pretty garden bits and bobs. Below, I created a makeshift shelf by resting an old scaffolding plank on bricks. When it comes to styling, add a few botanical prints along with rustic wooden crates and zinc buckets.

MAKE / PAPER PLANT POTS

Recycle your old gardening magazines by turning them into stylish plant pots. You'll need a magazine and a cylinder-shaped object to use as a mould (I used a small tumbler). Start by tearing out your chosen page and folding it in half vertically to make a long strip. Roll the strip tightly around the mould several times to create a cylinder, leaving extra paper at the base. Fold the paper in at the base to make a sturdy pot with no gaps for soil to fall through. You should now have a pot roughly 7.5-cm/3-inches high. Slide out the tumbler, fill your pot with potting compost/soil and it's ready for you to sow seeds or transplant seedings. These pots make great little gifts for garden lovers.

Wild Flowers of Europe

CREATE A TABLETOP GARDEN

A tabletop garden is a great way to showcase favourite plants and pots or seasonal displays. Use a pair of trestles or table legs and an old blackboard or reclaimed marble slab to make a table, then amass a collection of interesting plants with varying leaf shapes (here, gypsophila and *Ophiopogon planiscapus* 'Nigrescens') and add a mirror to double the impact of the display (opposite and above left). Any surface offers an opportunity for a mini display. An old bench is home to a hosta and two muehlenbeckias (left), while the roof of a log store carries a selection of containers planted with spring bulbs (above).

RECYCLED ELEMENTS

Bring personality to your space with salvaged items.

There are a few reasons that people incorporate recycled elements into their gardens. One is budget; often (but not always) recycled items are more affordable than new garden furniture, planters and decorative features. I'm talking about pieces that people might otherwise throw away – items salvaged from building sites, for example, such as rusty concrete reinforcement grids for a climber to scramble over, or defunct floorboards and pieces of masonry from which you could fashion a bench. Style is another reason to opt for recycled objects – you are likely to end up with something totally unique that's a real talking point. Finally, using salvaged items is eco-friendly and sustainable, as it keeps them out of landfill.

So where can you source such items? Be a magpie and look out for houses that are being refurbished, as skips/dumpsters are a good place to find things that can be reused (always check with the owners before taking things out of a skip). Good old car boot/yard sales are always worth a browse, or trawl online auction sites if you are hunting for something in particular, such as an old ceramic sink or zinc washing tub. If you have a slightly larger budget, salvage and reclamation yards will be your best bet. They are also promising places to source attractive gardenalia – vintage watering cans, old terracotta pots and galvanized metal bowls and trays that can be repurposed as attractive planters.

A NEW LEASE OF LIFE

Recycled items bring interest and charm to even the smallest outdoor space. A vase of garden flowers sits atop a vintage metal tray (below left), while an old bench in a shady spot is surrounded by salvaged planters (below centre), and a galvanized metal pan once used for animal feed has been put into service as a water butt – one to avoid if you have small children (below right). The low bench opposite was made from salvaged materials and is home to chunky pots and a metal mirror.

TOP TIP

Use recycled concrete blocks and an old plank to make a bench. Plant grasses behind, and it can double as a garden divider too.

INDUSTRIAL SALVAGE

Old wooden wine or fruit crates are so versatile (opposite). I used this example to display the cake at our wedding reception and now it's been put into service in the garden to show off a collection of cheerful spring bulbs in assorted containers. In early autumn, I plant up a selection of bulbs in various pots. In springtime, when the bulbs start to shoot, I gather the pots together and arrange them on top of the upturned crate with lanterns, urns and other bits and pieces of attractive gardenalia – it brightens the garden when not much else is in flower. A vintage sewing machine table with rusty metal planter and urn makes a striking vignette positioned against the black-stained wall of a shed (left).

MAKE / RECYCLED PLANTER

Old wooden crates are ideal for this project. A new crate will also work well and will soon age once exposed to the elements, but will benefit from treatment with a protective wood stain. If the crate has a solid base, you'll need to drill a few holes in it to allow for drainage. Now line the crate with black plastic sheeting. Fold it neatly into the corners (a bit like lining a cake pan) and use a staple gun to fix it in place. Add a thin layer of terracotta pot shards or broken-up polystyrene pieces to aid drainage. Fill the crate with the growing medium that best suits the plants you want to grow, then plant it up. I used white argyranthemums, *Nicotiana alata*, purple salvias and spider flower (*Cleome*).

VERTICAL DISPLAYS

Make the most of all available space - the sky's the limit!

Living walls have become a big trend in recent years and the idea of using all the available space in your garden works particularly well for those of us with more modest plots. As well as covering bare walls and fences with climbers, you can hang planters and display collections and interesting items. Debbie Smail, the owner of one of the gardens we visited while working on this book, collects vintage birdcages and has hung a growing collection of them on a black wood-clad wall in her garden – a blue passion flower (*Passiflora caerulea*) has begun to scramble around them (above right). Due to constant exposure to the elements, the metal of the cages has started to rust, which only adds to their charm.

On a brick wall in the same garden (above left), a vintage galvanized metal bathtub and bowl hang side by side, creating an attractive decorative feature in their own right as they wait to be planted up. There are so many different items you could use to decorate your garden walls: old street signs, shelving units, oversized china platters and wall planters are all good options. I once stumbled across an old rusty street sign at a flea market that had 'Selina Terrace' on it...of course, I had to buy it, and it now adorns a wall in our garden, forming a backdrop to our outdoor living area. I'm now busy searching for something equally unique that has my husband's name on it!

UP ON THE ROOF

Danish garden designer Dorthe Kvist saw a sunny spot on the roof of an outbuilding as a gardening opportunity. She made raised beds and planted them with vegetables and edible flowers that encourage bees and other insect life. The beds are accessed via a ladder. If you want to try this, ask a builder to check that your roof can bear the weight of planters.

BULWELL NOTTM

MAKE / PRETTY PANSY THEATRE

Talented gardener Debbie Smail designed this plant theatre to display potted plants such as pansies (*Viola x wittrockiana*). You can either revamp an old shelving unit or make one from a crate (opposite). Paint the shelves with black exterior wood paint or stain, then make the scallop-edged roof. Debbie used a strip of code 3 lead (from eBay) and a cup as a template for the semi circles along one edge. Cut along the scalloped edge with scissors (these were easier to use than a craft knife, but were blunted by the end). Mould the lead to the roof of the theatre and tack it in place using a hammer and galvanized nails. Hang the shelves on a sunny wall and arrange your pots of pansies.

STYLE TIP

This pretty styling idea will jazz up any garden fence and is a great decorative detail for parties or other get-togethers. Wind a length of string around the neck of a small glass bottle or jar and secure it tightly with a double knot. Now thread another length of string under the first and wind it around the fence post several times before securing with a knot. Once all the bottles/jars are fixed in place, use a watering can to fill each one with water and then pop in a couple of flowers or herbs. No fence? Push sturdy sticks into the ground along a path edge and tie your bottles/jars onto them instead.

TRULY TINY GARDENS

Windowsills, window boxes and hanging displays.

Outdoor space is a valued commodity nowadays, but clever use of containers can transform even the smallest patch into a leafy oasis. Be creative and work with what you've got, whether it's a pocket-sized internal courtyard or narrow balcony. Window boxes are one of my favourite features for compact spaces, as they can be enjoyed from both inside and out. Although most often used for flowering plants, they are versatile – you can use them to grow herbs (perfect for outside a kitchen window) and even fruit and vegetables such as alpine strawberries and cherry tomatoes.

There are a variety of different designs out there, but my top tip is to measure your windowsill before buying a window box to make sure it will fit comfortably (if you have very shallow sills, you can fit metal brackets to the wall under the window to hold the box). Here (above right), an antique metal planter with a decorative edging has been planted with cheerful red pelargoniums that stand out against the black cladding of the wall behind. If you have deep windowsills, you could line up a collection of different pots (above left). I like to position a row of pots containing different varieties of lavender outside our windows during the summer months, as the plant is said to repel flies. It's also a joy to throw open the window on a warm day and breathe in the heady scent of lavender (opposite above right).

MAKING THE MOST OF YOUR OUTSIDE SPACE

When you're short on outside space, window boxes and hanging planters are a wonderful way to introduce more greenery into your plot. A surprisingly large number of different plants will thrive in a window box, and for an ever-changing seasonal display you can plant them up with perennials plus a selection of annual flowers that can be replaced as they fade. To keep a small courtyard, tiny terrace or balcony garden uncluttered, try positioning your containers off the ground to create an illusion of greater floor space. Attach planters to sunny walls, suspend hanging baskets from hooks and place window boxes on a deep ledges or fix them to wall brackets.

Hanging planters are another way to add interest to a small space and make the most of walls and other vertical surfaces. There are so many different styles, from woven wicker baskets to modern metal containers. Choose a design that you love and that suits your budget and garden, and remember that you'll need a wall-mounted bracket or hook to hang the planter from. I have wicker baskets and plant them with *Narcissus* 'Tête-à-tête' bulbs and trailing ivy. In the summer I then plant annual bedding plants such as Surfinia double-flowered petunias on top of the bulbs, and when these fade I replace them with winter pansies in the autumn (above left). These flower pretty much the whole way through the winter and then by springtime the narcissus bulbs start to shoot up again. Every year I replace the top layer of the compost/soil to keep the nutrient levels topped up. Hanging planters do tend to dry out fast, so position yours within easy reach, otherwise watering them becomes a chore.

Styling gardenalia is all about using your creativity to bring a little vintage magic into your garden. Use pieces of careworn furniture, such as side tables with peeling paint, as plant stands (above). Store vintage pots in old crates while they are waiting to be used. Old tins also make great storage boxes for seed packets, and vintage baskets can hold balls of string and garden tools (left).

VINTAGE GARDENALIA

Vintage pieces will add charm to any outside space.

The term 'gardenalia' describes vintage collectibles related to gardens and gardening, and these are my favourite items to scout around for at car boot/yard sales, flea markets and reclamation yards. Some of my best finds include beautiful galvanized metal watering cans, a lichen-encrusted antique statue and a French metal bistro table and chairs set that had turned alluringly rusty with the passage of time. Look out for old metal washtubs, watering cans and pails (opposite). They don't have to be in perfect condition – it's a bonus if there are rusty holes in the base, as it saves you drilling new ones for drainage.

Ageing metal gates look great propped up against a wall as a support for climbing plants, as do old metal cart wheels. A birdcage makes for a quirky planter and even weathered tools can be turned into a feature. Sourcing such items is great fun; you might spy an unusual piece and have a place for it instantly, or you could buy it and let it adorn your garden until inspiration strikes.

TOP TIP

Styling your gardenalia is easy – use some of the pieces to create decorative vignettes in little nooks around your garden.

THE ABC OF GARDENING
W. E. SHEWELL COOPER

SHED SCENE

The walls of this cute shed have been painted in Kitchen Green by the Little Greene Paint Company. It's the perfect backdrop for plants, zinc pails and a director's chair (a lucky eBay find). The chair is positioned at the back of the shed and is the ideal spot for a moment of contemplation or to sit out a sudden rain shower.

MAKE / STENCILLED BUCKETS

Sometimes you can strike lucky and find vintage pieces with interesting stamps, lettering or initials stencilled onto them that offer clues as to their past lives. It's a decorative touch that you can easily replicate by adding your own chosen words or phrases to an old pail or planter using a stencil letter kit (these can be found on the internet). I printed the word FLEURS onto two vintage metal buckets. To stencil your word, you'll need a small stippling brush and some white exterior paint. Don't overload the brush with paint - it needs to be fairly dry to get a good effect. And make sure you wait until one letter has dried before you start the next one, to avoid smudging.

URBAN HERBS

If space is an issue, herbs are the perfect solution, as they will happily grow in containers. This sheltered spot is ideal for an array of different types, including rosemary and fennel. Old metal buckets create a uniform effect that doesn't detract from the planting.

TOP TIP

Mismatched seating brings quirky charm to this romantic, semi-wild town garden. Find similar pieces at car boot/yard sales and flea markets.

When it comes to choosing garden furnishings, work with what you already have – don't be afraid to mix different chairs around an existing table, for example. If you are in the market for a few new pieces, try them out for comfort before you buy, and do your research into how they will cope with the elements.

CHOOSING FURNITURE

Finding the right pieces for your outdoor space.

These days there is a huge array of garden furniture to choose from, with DIY stores and even supermarkets offering different ranges. Before you buy anything, think about the way you use your outdoor space. Do you like to eat outside during the warmer months? If so, a table and chairs will be top of your list. If you have a tiny space, could you slot in a bench or folding chairs and a table? Anyone who does a lot of entertaining might want a garden sofa.

Your budget will, of course, dictate where and what you buy. Do you need to invest in something new or could you revamp something you already own? I'm a great believer in mixing old with new. We call this part of our garden (left) the middle patio, and this summer I used a vintage French metal table and a wooden table once employed as a desk to create one long table. The chairs are a combination of old wood and metal folding chairs, Indian woven stools and rattan chairs by Bloomingville from & Hobbs. When positioning furniture, make sure there's enough room for guests to sit around a table comfortably. Once you have your furniture in place, you can do the fun part – style the tabletop with potted plants and vases of freshly picked flowers.

SUIT YOUR SPACE

Vintage-style cast-iron designs (opposite) bring the right vibe to a blowsy cottage garden, while this streamlined contemporary table and chairs set works well on a modern deck. Lightweight rattan or cane seating can be brought in or out as the weather dictates.

DECORATIVE DETAILS

Using quirky elements to add something special.

Just as with interiors, it's often the smaller details and finishing touches that really enhance a garden. While working on this book, I picked up more than a few new decorative ideas from the lovely gardeners I met along the way. They generously passed on a multitude of clever styling tips that I can now share with you. After visiting Lou Grace's beautiful garden and spotting her sturdy old TAC spade, I was thrilled to find a similar spade with a wooden handle at a car boot sale and rushed home to plunge it among the perennials in our herbaceous border! Lanterns are an atmospheric way to bring light into your garden. Use oil lamps or candle lanterns and hang them from shepherd's crooks lining a garden path. Creating homes for wildlife is another way of introducing decorative details into the garden as well as encouraging birds and insects to shelter and nest. We had a family of blue tits nesting in our bird box this year and it was a joy to watch mum and dad popping in and out of the tiny hole bearing flies and grubs to feed their offspring. The boxes look good attached to our plum tree too – win win!

FINISHING TOUCHES

A grouping of vintage glass bottles creates a pleasing vignette by an old metal gate (below left), while a shallow dish filled with rainwater provides a decorative detail and doubles as a bird bath (below). Hunt down garden finds at country fairs and shows (opposite left, below left and right). Handmade rusted metal poppy heads add support to a patch of *Verbena bonariensis* (opposite above right).

TAC

STYLE TIP

Position a bird table so that you have a good view of it and can watch local birdlife come and go. This traditional pedestal bird table is sited in the centre of a metal arch that cleverly draws your eye down the garden (above). Storage is vital, whatever size your plot, and allows you to hide away less-attractive essentials such as bags of potting soil. This beehive-inspired storage box is both practical and pretty (right).

MAKE / BUG HOTEL

Attract wildlife into your garden with a bug hotel. You'll need some wooden offcuts, a saw, an electric screwdriver, screws, chicken wire, a hammer and tacks, natural materials such as moss, pine cones and lengths of bamboo, and a piece of metal sheeting. Position the pieces of wood on a flat surface and form a house shape with a few internal divisions, sawing the wood to size. The roof pieces will need an angle cut to form a gable. Screw the house together. Cut a piece of chicken wire to fit the back, tack it into place and fill the divisions with natural materials before covering the front of the house with more chicken wire. Make the roof by folding the metal sheet over the gable and using the hammer to create the fold. Screw the roof in place and hang the bug hotel as desired.

MAKE / BIRD BOX

To make this rustic bird house, you'll need a birch log, wooden offcuts for the base, roof and back support, a drill bit, a hammer and chisel, and an electric screwdriver and screws. First hollow out the log by drilling holes into the top and using the hammer and chisel to carve out the central core. Using the drill bit, make an entrance hole near the top of the log. Screw a base, roof and back panel to the log and fix the back support to a sturdy post or tree.

OUTDOOR LIGHTING

For when the sun goes down.

Metal-framed lanterns with tea lights inside light the way up wooden steps (above left). A solar-powered string of lights draped over a bamboo wigwam makes a good job of lighting a pathway (above right), and battery-powered mini string lights wrapped around pots of succulents bring an inviting glow to an outdoor seating area (opposite).

Inside, we use lighting to add drama, create mood and illuminate important tasks, and it can be employed in exactly the same way in the garden. There are lots of outdoor lighting options, which can be temporary or permanant fixtures. If you are planning a garden from scratch, you can add integrated lighting, such as wall lights and spotlights to light up pathways or trees. Solar-powered lights, which come in all shapes and sizes, are an easy 'unfitted' alternative. Position them in your borders or use them to outline paths and other features. Solar outdoor string lights are great for parties – hang them in swags against walls or trellising, or hook them up to create a shape or spell a name. Battery-powered outdoor lights also add a magical glow. I like to illuminate my favourite gardenalia to make a feature of it – group items together and drape string lights around them, hiding the battery pack. Don't forget the magical beauty of candlelight: use candle lanterns either side of your door, to light a path, hanging from a tree or as an atmospheric table centrepiece.

TOP TIP

Outdoor battery string lights add sparkle to pots and containers, and you can hide the battery pack under the foliage.

STYLE TIP

Neon is a popular choice for statement lighting and now companies like Love Inc. are making LED outdoor versions. Here (left and opposite) I used a pink neon heart to create a fashion-led scheme for an outdoor table. I centred the neon heart on the table, as I like the way it casts a warm pink glow, and used painterly plates by Royal Doulton. I continued the look with pink candles along the table and in lanterns. Look to online companies for unusual garden lighting. Lights4fun is my other go-to for solar-powered string lights and exterior LED filament bulbs.

MAKE / POMPOM LANTERNS

For these lanterns, you'll need 18- or 20-gauge craft wire, wire cutters, a clean glass/Mason jar and some pompom trim. I used Ball preserving jars because the embossed logo creates a pretty candlelit pattern. Wrap a length of wire around the neck of the jar as tightly as you can and twist the ends together securely. Snip off the end of the wire. Add a handle by attaching a longer length of wire to the wire on one side of the neck. Loop it over to the opposite point and twist to secure. Wrap the pompom trim around the neck of the jar, tie the two ends together and snip the excess. Place a tea light in the jar, light it and you're all set for a pretty display when the sun goes down.

BRINGING THE
OUTSIDE IN

FORAGING FROM YOUR GARDEN

Enjoy foliage and flowers gathered from your outside space.

Gathering flowers from the garden allows you to create seasonal bouquets and pretty gifts that are unique, organic and budget friendly. You'll also find foliage and flowers that are not available in your average florist. In our garden we have a *Magnolia grandiflora* tree and every year I cut a couple of branches when they are covered with fragrant white flowers. Springtime also gives us primroses, lilacs and the most beautiful apple blossom.

The best time to cut flowers is in the morning, before the sun is too hot. Fill a bucket with water to give flowers a drink as soon as they have been cut. Use sharp secateurs (or loppers for woody branches) and make clean cuts at an angle. Be selective about where you chop – cuts just after a bud or growth point on the stem won't damage the plant. However, it's better to take a stem or two from lots of different plants rather than decimating one particular specimen. Before you bring your haul inside, check for any bugs and gently shake them off.

Planning ahead is key: I plant extra bulbs in autumn so that in spring I can cut some to decorate our home while leaving lots to be enjoyed in the garden. If you're sowing seeds for annuals such as sweet peas, you'll need to start thinking about these a good six months before their flowering peak in high summer.

GIFTS FROM THE GARDEN

Foraging for flowers is one of the best things about having a garden. Spanish bluebells wait patiently to be picked from the border (top left). Another favourite of mine is phacelia, which looks lovely arranged in a glass vase with argyranthemums (top right). White lacecap hydrangea pops against a dark backdrop (below left), and Japanese flowering cherry blossom is a visual treat in spring (below right). Cut sprigs don't last for long, so enjoy their beauty while you can (opposite).

CREATIVE RECYCLING

When trees and shrubs in our garden need cutting back or pruning, I always save a few stems or branches for inside the house. The rest is cut up and put on the compost heap. Use tall ceramic or enamel jugs for displaying larger branches and refresh the water every couple of days.

MAKING AN ENTRANCE

I love to use flowers to create a sense of welcome at home. Our Seletti pink neon light casts a warm pink glow over flowers from the garden arranged in a vase on our retro chest of drawers. The posy includes foxgloves (my favourites), with a branch from a crab apple tree adding a little drama to the space.

STYLE TIP

A great way to bring the outside in is by using green, the colour of nature, to paint your walls and skirting/base boards. Here, even a wooden cupboard has been given a lick of paint in the same shade. The botanical feel is enhanced with outdoor furniture – vintage garden chairs made from metal and wood and a bamboo armchair that has been spray-painted bright green. The bottle vases make great vessels for displaying foxgloves and sweet peas, among other things, and the seagrass rug adds to the natural vibe.

SEASONAL ARRANGEMENTS

The joy of beautiful blooms all year round.

Bringing flowers and foliage in from your garden to enhance your home decor is a simple detail that makes a big impact, whether you're in need of a table centrepiece for a special occasion, a welcoming display for a hallway table or something just to bring a smile to your face. Flowers make us feel good and each season offers a new wave of blooms that can be enjoyed inside and out.

Think about what vessels you have to hand. Often I choose a vase or container before heading into the garden, then cut the required number of stems to the exact length to fit the chosen vessel. Other times I wander out and cut plants on a whim, seeing what's available and abundant, then decide on a vase once I have a handful of freshly cut flowers. Whichever way you like to do things, chances are that you're going to need plenty of vases and other containers to be used in different rooms in your home and at various times of the year. Sometimes a vase will only hold short stems, so it's a good idea to invest in a selection of small bud vases, as well as containers that will house a larger bouquet. I tend to source my vases from flea markets, garden and plant shops, supermarkets and antiques shops.

When it comes to arranging flowers, I don't have any rules as such – I like loose, natural-looking posies and am drawn to colour palettes that I find appealing and that will sit well with my interior. During autumn, I forage for

CELEBRATE THE CHANGING SEASONS

Each season brings its own beautiful new botanicals. This crab apple blossom has an amazing scent – the tree belongs to my lovely neighbour, who gave me permission to cut what I liked (opposite left). These colourful summer blooms in pinks, blue and bright orange are all home-grown cut flowers (opposite right). I added a few grasses and loosely arranged the whole lot in a vintage bucket. In autumn, dried seed heads are my go-to for arrangements (above left). During the winter months, I bring in evergreen foliage – for extra twinkle, intersperse vases with tea lights (above right).

rosehips, branches laden with mini crab apples and big blousy dahlias (I love delicate peachy pink 'Café au Lait'). In winter, I look for evergreens and berries and mix them with dried flowers and seed heads saved from summer. After the winter months, joyful pops of vibrant colour from flowering spring bulbs are really uplifting. A jolly display of blossom with narcissus, anemones and lilacs is mood enhancing and I also gather flower-laden branches from blossoming apple trees – the scent is heavenly.

Then, of course, the summer months are when flowers are at their most abundant. If you're growing your own cut flowers, you might have a glut of blooms at some point during the season. Whenever this happens, I cut the surplus flowers and pop them in vintage galvanized metal buckets filled with water, then arrange these by a doorway, at the bottom of the staircase or along a hallway – it creates a sense of walking through a flower garden and is a striking idea for bringing the outside in.

RHUBARB RHUBARB

What if your rhubarb has bolted? Well, it's not all bad news – rhubarb flowers are pretty, so just remove them and use them as a cut flower. This teak sideboard is a great place for large arrangements and the vintage 'Fleurs' botanical print continues the outdoors-in theme and makes a good backdrop for an unusual display.

TOP TIP

Home-grown stems look great popped into a vintage glass bottle. When several are grouped together, they make a striking floral display.

MAKE / DRIED FLOWERS

The art of preserving flowers dates back centuries. You can dry almost any flowers, seed heads or grasses by stripping off the leaves quickly after they have been cut. Tie them in a bunch and leave them to air-dry upside down for two to four weeks. If you grow your own flowers and have a glut of nigella, alliums or hydrangeas, pick some blooms especially for drying and using later to enhance an autumn or winter arrangement or a festive wreath. A shed entirely dedicated to drying flowers is wonderful but not essential - any dry space out of direct sunlight and with good air circulation will do the job.

MAKE / HOME GROWN BOUQUET

Select a good mixture of flowers - I chose peachy pink and cream David Austin roses mixed with chocolate cosmos, the prettily named love-in-a-mist (*Nigella*) seed heeds and bishop's weed (*Ammi majus*) flowers. Remove all leaves and thorns down to about 10 cm/4 inches below the flower heads then place the prepped flowers on a flat surface. Now, holding one stem in your hand, use your other hand to add more stems to it, rotating the flowers every time and adding new stems at a slight angle. Continue until you have used all the flowers, then tie the stems securely together with raffia or string. Snip off the ends of the stems so that they are all even, and find a suitable vase for the bouquet.

STYLE TIP

If you love the look of home-grown flowers but haven't got around to growing your own, do an internet search for a local flower grower and support their business by ordering blooms from them. My supplier is a lovely lady called Nicky (www.bucketsofblooms.co.uk) who grows beautiful seasonal British flowers in a field in Hampshire, UK. Her annual mallow flowers (*Lavatera*) are particularly divine!

If you've gone to the trouble of creating a beautiful place to grow your own flowers, be sure to label your plants (above). Keep plants supported with decorative wicker wigwams or metal garden obelisks and invest in a trug or basket for collecting your blooms (opposite). A workbench inside this pretty shed (left) is the perfect space to sort and arrange flowers, but a garden table will work as well.

CREATE A CUTTING GARDEN

Growing fragrant blooms and foliage especially for your home.

Growing flowers in a dedicated plot especially for cutting is a lovely luxury if you have the space, and it saves you from denuding or leaving gaps in your garden borders. Depending on the size of your outside space, flowers for cutting can be grown in tubs, large pots or empty spots in the border, but a raised bed is the ideal option, as they are easily accessible and have good drainage. You can buy treated wooden frames and kits from garden centres, or make your own if you have the skills and tools, using rot-resistant wood such as red cedar, black locust or redwood. Make sure you position your bed in a sunny site and that it's filled with weed-free, fertile soil.

When it comes to planting, choose cut-and-come-again plant varieties with long stems – they are better for cut flowers, as the more you pick, the more you get. Research how much space your plants will need to grow and what height they grow to – there's a fine line between overcrowding and growing plenty to cut and enjoy.

TOP TIP

A collection of glass vases makes a pretty centrepiece. Look in charity shops/thrift stores for tiny jugs, cut-glass vases and dainty tumblers.

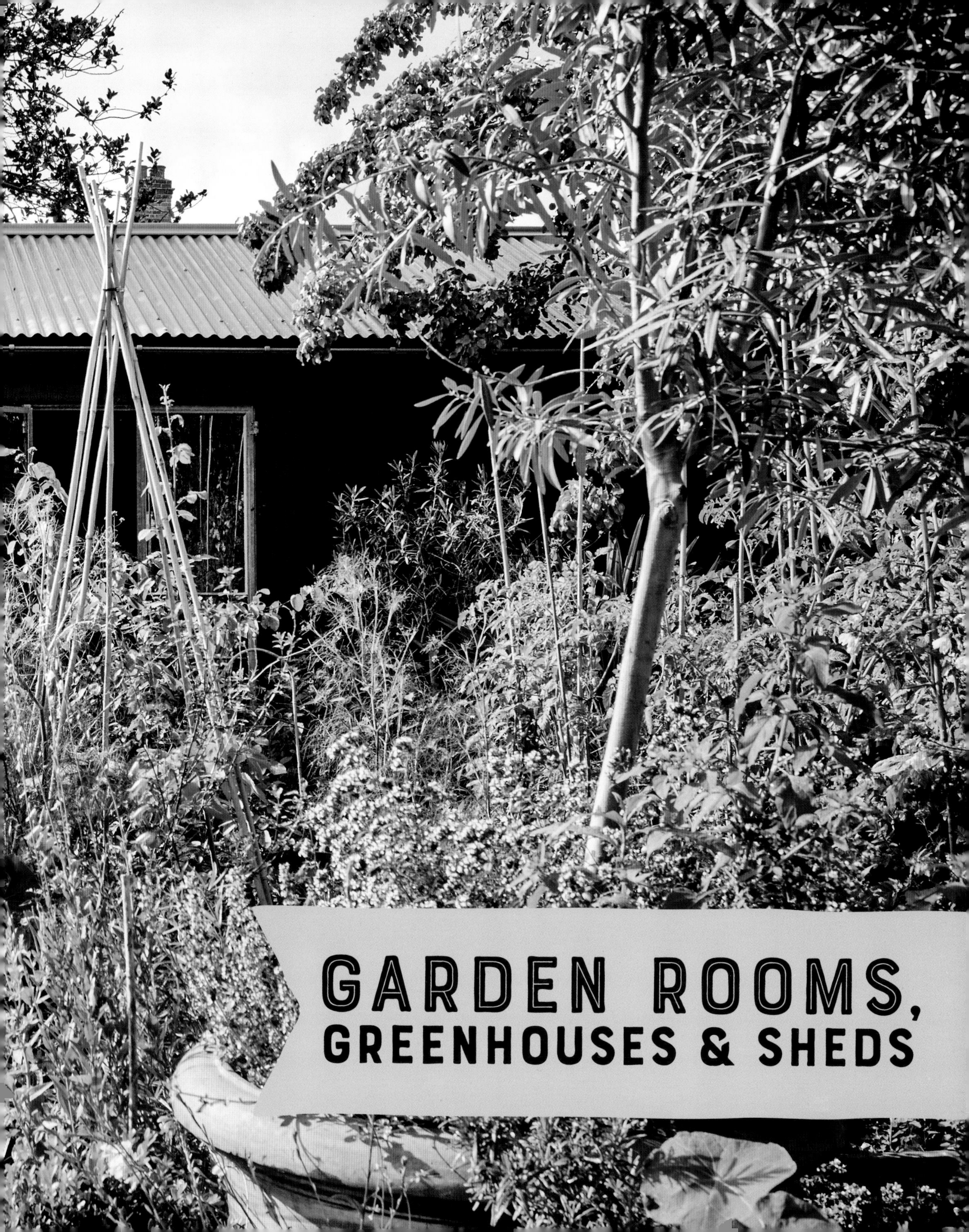

GARDEN ROOMS, GREENHOUSES & SHEDS

TOP TIP

Green glass bottle vases echo the many greens in the garden outside and bring a quirky botanical feel to this sleek modern space.

This contemporary steel and glass extension was designed by a Swedish architect to sit among the lush green garden foliage that surrounds it. It's a great way to be able to use the garden even on wet days. The interior has been styled with a simple monochrome palette and a leafy kentia palm (*Howea forsteriana*), which helps to blur the divisions between inside and out.

GARDEN ROOMS

Create extra entertaining, living and relaxation space.

More popular than ever, garden rooms are a useful addition to any outside space. They can be used as office spaces, crafting rooms, yoga studios or places to enjoy a million other activities. Often a separate structure or an extension/addition to a property, garden rooms can be made from most traditional building materials. You could adapt an existing building, such as a large shed, garage or greenhouse, or commission a new pod, cabin or summer house. Whatever you choose, it's essential to check that you have all the correct planning permissions before embarking on the project.

Once your garden room has been realized, you'll need to think about how you want to decorate and style the new space. Perhaps you would like the garden room to reflect the garden and have a verdant, naturalistic 'potting shed' vibe, or you could opt for something strikingly modern that contrasts with the garden that surrounds it. If it's intended to be a multipurpose space, it's advisable to factor in plenty of storage, and if you are intending to use the space all year round, invest in a wood-burning stove for the cooler months and some cosy elements such as extra blankets and rugs.

MAKE / BOTANICAL PRINTS

Making your own botanical artworks is easy if you have some paper, a printer and a device to print from. I like to print black-and-white images onto A4/US letter brown kraft paper, but you can use any colour or texture of paper you like (as long as it is compatible with your printer). Search online for free-usage vintage botanical images until you find something you like. Try and source the highest-resolution image possible, as then the print quality will be better. Save the image to your device, then make it black and white and send it to print. To create an attractive display, you could print a few different images and use bulldog clips to hang them onto tacks in the wall (opposite).

A PLACE TO DREAM

Surely everyone dreams of a little cabin hidden away at the bottom of the garden with space to write, create and relax? I know I do! This timber-clad Scandi-style cabin (above) was designed and built by stylist Rose Hammick's husband, Andrew. Recycled wood from delivery pallets was used for the walls, while the metal-framed windows and doors were salvaged from an old factory building. The sloping corrugated-metal roof allows rainwater to run into aluminium guttering that drains into a water butt. The collected water is then used to water the garden.

ENVELOPES

SEMI-WASHED
MANDHELING
ARABICA
CROP NEW CROP INDONESIA

CREATE A GARDEN RETREAT

You may already have a shed or outbuilding that could be transformed into a versatile social space instead of somewhere just to store the lawnmower and bikes. That's exactly what photographer Cathy Pyle has done. After clearing out her shed, she made a corner sofa from old wooden pallets, covered it with cushions from a cast-off sofa and knocked up a coffee table on casters to match. Old coffee sacks warm up the white-painted wooden walls and strings of lights add sparkle. Painting the exterior of a garden building black is a sure-fire way to make it disappear behind foliage and flowers in your garden, and it looks so chic.

THE GREENHOUSE

The perfect environment for plants that feel the cold.

There is something a little magical about a greenhouse. Due to their purpose – providing a stable, warm environment for plants – they tend to be comforting, cosy spaces and I feel happy whenever I'm surrounded by growing things. If you're a serious gardener, a greenhouse will allow you to grow from seed and to cultivate tender plants that can't survive outside over winter. They are a perfect example of how a practical space can also be appealing and inspiring. This beautiful example was built by Peter Wallin, a skilled carpenter, for his wife Lena (follow her on instagram @lenasskoghem). It's roomy enough for an armchair – somewhere to sit and enjoy the surroundings whenever there's a spare minute. One of my favourite features is the salvaged decorative window in the back wall, which provides a glimpse of the forest beyond (see overleaf). At the front are raised beds (also built by Peter), and a low willow fence borders the plot to one side. Decorative finishing touches include vintage metal watering cans and an old wooden barrel reused as a planter.

Of course, as with most garden buildings, a greenhouse will require maintenance and upkeep. If yours is made from wood, you'll need to treat the timber or repaint it at regular intervals. At the start of the growing season, give the windows a good wash and remove any fallen leaves or debris from the roof.

STYLE YOUR SPACE

Shelving is essential for any greenhouse – somewhere to store pots, tools and plant labels. It also provides a place to style gardening items and other bits and bobs to create a decorative vignette. If there is space, bring a table in and arrange a display of potted plants and other objects you find appealing. Having a greenhouse must be the ultimate garden goal – not only does it look wonderful, but it allows you to grow plants that need a warm climate in order to thrive. Lena Wallin's greenhouse is home to a fig, tomatoes and squash, while the glasshouse on this page nutures a flourishing grapevine.

GREENHOUSE GOALS

One of the most inspiring places I have visited is Rosendals Trädgård in Stockholm, Sweden – a garden foundation that espouses biodynamic farming practices and a 'farm to fork' concept. If you ever get the chance to visit, I highly recommend it. On site are three large greenhouses currently used as a shop, a café serving dishes made with their own produce and a space for weddings and parties. Their in-house florist uses the shelves in the large greenhouse to create an ever-changing floral display from whatever is in season. During the summer months you can pick your own flowers there too.

TOP TIP

While you're visiting gardens and garden centres, take photos of features you like, as you may be able to recreate some ideas in your own garden.

POTTING SHEDS

Pottering about in the shed is one of life's greatest pleasures.

ALL SORTED

The potting shed is the natural home for storing all sorts of miscellaneous garden equipment and accessories. Here, wooden seed crates and stacked terracotta pots wait to be used to house new plants (above). This space (opposite) is very versatile – it's a cross between a greenhouse and a shed, with houseplants flourishing alongside all the essentials needed for growing seedlings and potting on tender plants. The simple grey concrete floor and black walls give this shed an on-trend feel.

If you're a keen gardener but only have enough space for one structure in your garden, it has to be a potting shed. It will prove an invaluable garden headquarters – somewhere to store all those garden essentials, pot on seedlings and take shelter from the rain. There are many different styles of shed to choose from. Some have large windows or glass panels (enabling you to grow plants from seed), but all of them need a generously sized potting bench for you to work at.

When it comes to the exterior of your shed, you need to think about whether you want it to blend into your garden or provide a decorative feature. Using dark wood stain or paint will make any structure recede into the background and provides a dramatic contrast to green foliage. Pale or bright colours draw the eye and will make a shed stand out among garden greenery.

For me, sheds offer endless styling possibilities, which makes me very excited! I love arranging items on shelves and on the potting table purely to create a visually pleasing space that feels inspiring and is enjoyable to spend time in. To keep our shed clutter-free, we have a big old wooden cabinet to hold anything I don't want on show, as well as a weatherproof garden box outside the door. This came from Garden Trading and has a sloping metal roof – it's the perfect place for storing wellies/rubber boots, fish food and other garden equipment.

PRETTY PASTEL STYLE

I've admired this pastel shed owned by fellow author and stylist Jane Cumberbatch for many years and I've even had the pleasure of styling it for various photoshoots. It has a lovely rustic feel and is surrounded by established trees and planting. Roses, alliums and cardoons all create a country garden vibe.

STYLE TIP

Just after cutting a few blossom-laden boughs from my neighbour's crab apple tree (I did ask permission first), I plunged the stems straight into a bucket of water to give them a good drink (left). I like how the bucket looks on my potting bench – an Instagram opportunity might occur! It's good to appreciate garden moments as you busy yourself with horticultural tasks. Make a feature of drying bulbs by grouping them together and tying them with string, add a parcel tag to identify each variety and hang them on the wall of your shed (below).

A GOOD READ

I find vintage books on gardening fascinating reads and I like to collect them. Since my husband replaced the leaking roof of our shed, the space is weatherproof and my books can happily live here without getting damp. Secateurs are probably my most-used gardening tool and I couldn't resist buying this pair with pretty pale blue handles.

TOP TIP

If your potting shed is not a thing of beauty, paint or stain it black - it will be much less obtrusive - and pop a table in front to conceal it.

GO POTTY

Even if you don't have room for a potting shed, you might be able to squeeze a small potting bench into a corner of the garden. Essentially all you need is a sturdy and fairly weatherproof table to work on. For something more permanent, position the table against a wall and add a shelf or two above and large crates underneath for storage. This bench is home to towers of terracotta pots plus other attractive gardenalia and is the perfect place for repotting or dividing plants or arranging flowers on a sunny day (left).

DRESSING YOUR SHED

I love tracking down pretty 'accessories' for my shed, and by accessories I mean planters, urns and gardenalia – items like old trays, which are great for placing small pots on, lanterns, bottles and gardening books. Anything, really, that I think might work in the garden as a feature or that will look good on a shelf inside the shed. Hooks are super useful, as you always need something to hang tools and trugs from. I hunt for old brass hooks at car boot/ yard sales and junk shops, and vintage gardenalia at vintage fairs.

MAKE / SEED PACKETS

If you're collecting seeds, why not make your own seed packets? You'll need botanical illustrations (mine were from vintage wildflower books), access to a scanner, colour printer and computer, A4/US letter paper, scissors, PVA glue, washi tape and rub-down letters. Find a blank seed packet template on the internet and download it. Scan your chosen illustration (resize if necessary). Position the image on the template, then print. Following the instructions, cut out the packet and glue the flaps together, leaving the top of the envelope open. Insert your seeds and fold the top flap down to close. Seal the flap with a strip of washi tape and use rub-on letters to label the packet.

OTHER GARDEN ROOMS

This little tin shed (left) brings charm to a secluded corner of Debbie Smail's garden. It was made by salvage and vintage specialists The Old Yard from reclaimed corrugated metal sheets with a beautiful rusty patina. Inside, there is ample room for a writing desk or a comfy armchair and radio, making it a tranquil, cosy retreat. A shepherd's hut is a good option if you have a large garden, as they are a popular choice for glamping and guest accommodation. This one (opposite) was designed and built by Plankbridge Ltd, who are based in Dorset, UK.

STYLE TIP

A narrow windowsill is a good spot to show off blooms from the cutting patch (right). Line up glass jars along the ledge, half-fill each with water and pop in a couple of flowers (I used cosmos, sweet peas and marigolds). If you have an old chair, use this for a display – fill a bucket with water and flowers and place on the seat. Old wheelbarrows make interesting planters and can be moved around the garden to create new looks (above).

RELAXING OUTDOORS

OUTDOOR LIVING ROOMS

Taking indoor style outside.

Our outdoor living space is my favourite spot in our garden. I wanted to create a simple Scandinavian look, so opted for a clean, pared-down palette of black, grey and white, teaming it with natural materials such as wood, rattan and wicker. Create a cosy seating area just as you would indoors by using a rug to create a focal point and positioning furniture in a sociable cluster around it (durable weatherproof modular sofa sets are easy to find in department stores or big-box stores). Be ready for when the sun goes down with string lights overhead, and candles in lanterns on the coffee table.

Lush green wisteria foliage and leafy hydrangea, lavender and toabcco plants in zinc containers and dark grey stone pots add scent and interest to my outdoor living room. I gave our tired wooden decking a facelift with black wood stain and like to dress the sofa and armchairs with comfy cushions and throws, just as I do inside (opposite).

MAKE / VELVET CUSHION

Velvet adds a luxurious touch and here I've chosen green to tone with the foliage (opposite). You'll need two 48-cm/19-inch squares of fabric, sewing thread, 35-cm/14-inch zip and 45-cm/18-inch cushion pad. Pin the right sides of the squares together and tack/baste along one edge, taking a 1-cm/½-inch seam allowance. Stitch from each corner for 5 cm/2 inches. Lay the zip right side down on the wrong side of the seam. Tack/baste then stitch the zip in place. Remove tacking/basting and open the zip. With right sides facing, pin and stitch the remaining three sides together. Snip diagonally across the corners to reduce bulk. Turn right side out and insert the cushion pad.

OUTDOOR SUN TRAP

If space allows, position furniture in different areas of your garden to have somewhere to enjoy the sun throughout the day. This corner sofa (opposite), set against a backdrop of wisteria and pots of plantain lilies and baby's breath, is positioned to catch the last of the day's sun in this Danish garden.

MAKE / A BREEZE-BLOCK SOFA

This idea came from Instagrammer Cat Persson who created an easy-to-build sofa from recycled breeze/cinder blocks and wooden planks, without using any tools. Stack blocks on a flat surface (ideally two blocks high - any higher and the stack could become unstable) and lay planks on top (short scaffolding boards are ideal). Scatter with cushions and surround with pots - here we've used heuchera, sneezeweed, senecio and box.

MODERN DECKS

Transform a decked area into a relaxing outdoor room.

If installing a new decked area, research the different types of wood available – for example, larch wood is often chosen for its durability and can be laid and left untreated. In a couple of years it will have weathered and turned a beautiful silvery grey. For an existing decked area in need of a revamp, you could apply a coat of exterior wood stain to revive tired planks. If the expanse of wood feels too dominant, try cutting out planter pockets – I like to use fragrant and calming plants such as lavender in relaxing spaces. Adding pots to your deck will also link the space to the rest of your garden and for shade you could add a potted tree (olive trees grow well in large containers).

Illustrator Mhairi-Stella's garden backs onto the River Wey and she and her husband have created this idyllic decked area on the riverbank. Adjustable wooden sun loungers are ideal in this space, while a conifer hedge acts as a windbreak and offers privacy. Pots of delicate violas, lavender and catmint decorate the decking, and a storm lantern provides a gentle light in the evening.

This riverside deck (above) is at the bottom of a long garden, so it's essential to carry with you all that's required for an afternoon in the sun, watching the boats go by. I'm a huge fan of these basket bags (opposite bottom right), as they are practical, durable and stylish, and you can't have too many! I source mine via basketbasket.co.uk and lepapillonvert.co.uk.

BLACK-&-WHITE STYLING

I love the way Scandinavian friends often keep to a simple palette of black, white and grey outside. Black works well as a backdrop for natural elements (see how it complements the bamboo and olive tree opposite), so introduce it via furniture, dividers and planters, and throw in some black-and-white striped cushions.

STYLE TIP

This roofed decking area has been styled using natural colours and textures with slouchy calico-covered wood-framed deck chairs, a wicker coffee table and untreated wood decking. The inbuilt outdoor fireplace makes the space usable in the cooler months or on summer evenings after the sun has gone down. Introduce cosy elements such as soft blankets and flickering candlelight to complete the scene.

TOP TIP

Make your own storm lanterns in oversized, wide-necked glass jars by layering stones or gravel in the base and placing a pillar candle on top.

Candles add to the *hygge* vibe (above). Naked flames need a sheltered spot, but lanterns can be used even on breezier evenings. Keep seating relaxed and comfy by piling up cushions and blankets, as with this two-seater sofa under the shade of an apple tree (right). An outdoor log-burning stove (opposite) will keep you cosy on cooler days (and you can toast marshmallows!).

COSY CORNERS

Add a little garden *hygge* to create the perfect outdoor room.

Taking time to relax and unwind is highly important to our physical and mental health and wellbeing. To this end, I like to adopt the Danish ethos to create *hygge* in the garden. *Hygge* is the word the Danish use to describe a certain atmosphere prevalent in their homes and way of life – it's a combination of lifestyle, styling and feel-good time with friends and family, and it's certainly a relaxing concept. To carry this through to your outside space, the most essential item you need to make a cosy garden nook is comfy seating. Lightweight bamboo sofas partnered with generously padded cushions are a good choice and are a favourite among the Scandinavians, with companies like Tine K Home, Bloomingville and IKEA all stocking bamboo garden furniture ranges. Create your hideaway in a private space, under a weeping tree or in a private corner of the garden. The secluded nook shown opposite is nestled among fig, birch and rose trees, and surrounded by lower-growing honesty and hydrangeas.

SECLUDED RELAXATION

The heavenly scent of mock orange blossom makes this an idyllic spot for a small table and two armchairs. If your garden has two nearby trees with thick, sturdy trunks, put them to good use. In the shade of a cobnut tree, half-hidden by ferns (opposite), a cushioned hammock invites you to escape, with a sawn-off log providing a perch for a book and mug.

OUTDOOR BATHING

Alfresco cleansing relaxes and revives even the weariest soul.

ALL THE NECESSITIES FOR OUTDOOR BATHING

Natural organic products are ideal for using outside, as there are no nasty chemicals to splash on to nearby plants (above left). Add hooks in a handy position for towels, and a small stool or table is useful for storage. Plant climbers, such as passion flower (above centre), to soften the slatted walls enclosing an outdoor shower. A shallow metal pan works well as a water scoop for hair washing (above right). Hydrangeas and ferns are a good planting choice around your outdoor bathroom (opposite), as they thrive in moist conditions.

When it comes to creating garden rooms, we don't immediately think of installing an outdoor bathroom, but could there be anything more cleansing and relaxing than showering or bathing surrounded by nature, with a view of the garden and open sky?

In this garden, the shower's water supply comes via a pipe from a water tank housed on a nearby flat roof, where the sun heats it through the day. This means that 4–7pm on a sunny day is the best time for a warm shower. The tub, on the other hand, is a cold-water affair and is invigorating on a hot summer's day (but only for the brave when the weather is less kind). Make screens from dense climbing plants, fences or bamboo screening, and to keep the space feeling tranquil, opt for natural materials wherever possible. This corner of the garden is made private and secluded with lush Dutchman's pipe vine scaling the walls and pots of mophead hydrangeas, ferns and peonies surrounding the tub. If the water from the shower or tub will drain directly into the surrounding borders, remember to use chemical-free cleansing products (I like the organic range by Swedish company L:A Bruket). Non-slip wooden decking is kind to bare feet (check to ensure it is free from splinters) and allows water to drain into the ground below.

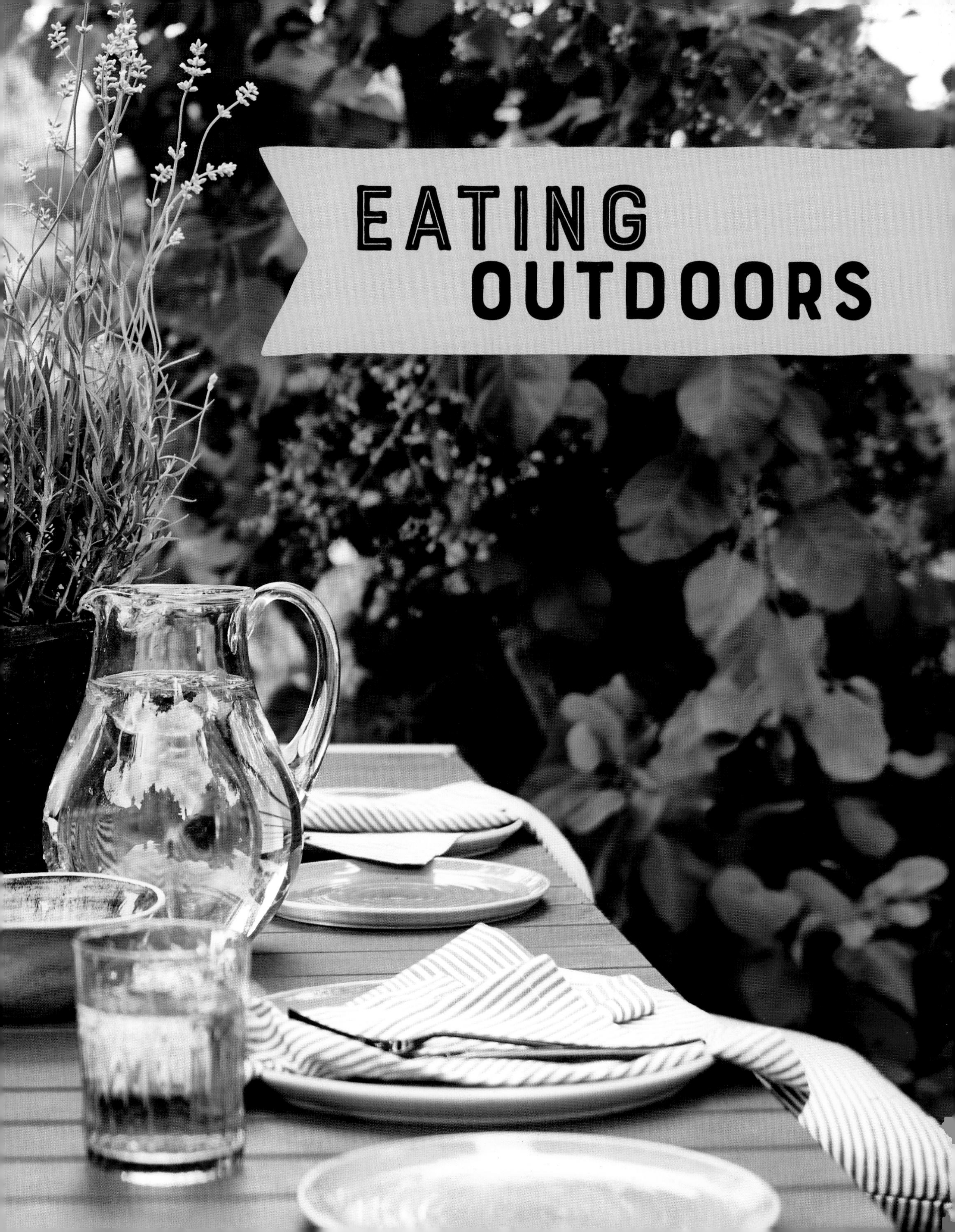
EATING
OUTDOORS

WEEKEND ENTERTAINING

Make the most of sunny days by socializing outside.

As we mow the lawn, tidy shrubs and fill the borders with flowering plants, it's often with thoughts of using the garden on warm days to welcome gatherings of friends and family. As soon as the weather allows, be ready to transform your garden into a social hub.

To keep the event relaxed and informal, serve drinks in large glass drinks dispensers so that your guests can help themselves, positioning the dispensers on wooden boxes or crates to give them extra height and make it easier for pouring. Don't forget to add a bucket of ice alongside if it's a particularly hot day.

Encourage your guests to linger at the table by adding comfy cushions to wooden or metal chairs and adding cosy throws if there is a chill in the air. If serving food, opt for wooden bowls and boards with a collection of enamelware to continue the simple, rustic style. Although it makes more laundry, I like to use cotton or linen napkins, which add to the organic mood.

And why not take the outside experience to the next level and extend the outdoor activities to include the laborious task of washing the dishes? Creating an outdoor washing-up station certainly makes the job more fun and everyone will want to help. I set up a table in the shade of the apple tree, with a large enamel bowl and a pitcher filled with warm soapy water (a clean watering can would also work well, and maintain the outdoor theme).

KEEP IT CASUAL

Move your table to the sunniest spot in the garden and pile plates, cutlery/flatware and napkins in the centre, rather than laying place settings. Wooden chopping boards and bowls feel right in these surroundings. Continue the garden theme with a vase of flowers – I've added sweet peas and roses in a clear glass bottle.

A PEACEFUL LUNCH SETTING

This grey slatted four-seater dining table set from online retailer Wayfair looks like painted wood, but is in fact made from polywood, which means it's weather resistant. I've styled the table for a family lunch with a calming colour palette of greys, greens and black, echoing the tones of the foliage in the background. Once you have selected the position for your table, look at the colours surrounding it – you might have lots of pink blooms or all green, or a dominant wall – and use these as the starting point for your table theme, bringing out items from the house that might fit with the setting. Here, pots of lavender and nicotiana continue the green theme.

STYLE TIP

Place a plant or flowers on a garden table to make it an inviting place to stop and sit. If your table is set against a backdrop of blooms, snip some stems for a vase and this will instantly make the table feel 'at home' in the space. I added a vibrant pink peony and a stately foxglove to a wide-necked glass storage jar with a few stems of greenery to link the table setting to the hedge beyond (above). The vibrant colours are a perfect contrast to the cool white enamelware.

Dorthe's dining table was made using trestles from IKEA topped with wide salvaged planks of timber (right). She has partnered the table with stackable aluminium Luxembourg chairs by Frédéric Sofia for French brand Fermob. These are a reinterpretation of the legendary chairs of Jardin du Luxembourg, originally created in 1923 for the parks of Paris. Available in 24 colours, you can mix or match as desired.

INDOOR/OUTDOOR DINING

Find ways to use your outside space all year round.

Danish garden designer Dorthe Kvist created this terrace dining room on the decked area next to her kitchen. The idea for an enclosed space came to her as a solution to the location – her house is situated on a hill and the terrace is west facing, so dining outside can be a windswept experience.

Dorthe and her husband built the walls using old windows salvaged from friends who were throwing them out after a house renovation. While the main purpose of these walls is to act as a windbreak, a welcome side effect is that they also serve as a greenhouse on the south-facing wall, providing shelter and warmth, and making this an ideal spot to grow tomatoes. An olive tree, underplanted with thrift, also thrives in this sheltered nook. The frames and structure have been painted black and white, and solar-powered festoon lights from Lights4Fun have been swagged across the windows to make the space usable into the evening. On the open side of this structure, Dorthe created a large long plant box where she grows herbs. This also doubles as a railing, separating the area from the lower-level garden below. Dorthe dreams of one day roofing the whole structure with glass, for use all year round.

TOP TIP
On this metal trolley Dorthe displays jars filled with shells and pebbles, while metal trays house pots of aeonium and Australian ivy.

MAKE / FLORAL PRINT NAPKINS

A fun way to preserve memories of summer. I use verbena, geraniums, marigolds, sweet peas, rose petals and yellow loosestrife, plus fruits such as cherries and raspberries, to provide vibrant splashes of pink and red. Cut 50-cm/20-inch squares of linen or 100% cotton fabric and dampen in water. Lay a square on a flat surface and place flowers and fruits (which can be broken up) over the wet fabric, then roll up from one side, trapping the flowers and fruits. Place on a wooden board and bash vigorously with a hammer to break up the petals and fruits. Unroll the fabric, shake off the flowers and fruits and hang the napkin up to dry. When dry, hem on all sides, then iron to fix the colours. Wash on a cool wash after use.

HWILA

STYLE TIP

A simple wooden table surrounded by slatted chairs can be elevated to a beautiful dining space with vases of garden flowers of varying heights along the length of the table. Here, the tallest central vase includes alliums and peonies with grasses and ferns, while the smaller vases contain catmint, marguerites and fiddleneck. Terracotta pots of pelargoniums complete the scene.

This classic dining table and chairs set just gets better the more it is weathered (left); for a similar set, look at Swedish company Grythyttan Stålmöbler. Coriander/cilantro, parsley, rosemary and salad leaves stand at the ready for adding to a dish (above). These stainless-steel shelves are a good choice for outside as they won't rust, and wicker baskets provide useful storage.

OPEN-AIR KITCHEN

Outdoor cooking and alfresco feasts.

Garden kitchens are so popular, even in countries where weather suitable for alfresco dining is not guaranteed. If budget allows, you could install a fully working kitchen with all the conveniences of an indoor kitchen. The possibilities are endless and there are plenty of companies offering a complete design service – Dutch company WWOO, for example, uses concrete shelving in lots of their designs and incorporates everything you need for creating an outdoor feast, including the kitchen sink.

Here in Sweden, Anna Malm has created a space for her family to cook and relax together. Her outdoor counter is positioned on the wall of her indoor kitchen, allowing the plumbing to be extended to the outdoor sink. If you love cooking outside but are not keen to make a permanent investment, set up a temporary kitchen space just for the summer – use a metal shelving unit or trolley to house crockery and utensils, place a table next to your barbecue as a worktop and surround the area with pots of herbs.

TOP TIP

Position your outdoor kitchen in an area of your garden that is partially covered so that the space can be used in most weathers.

GROWING YOUR OWN

Because nothing tastes as good as home-grown.

THE SATISFACTION OF SELF-SUPPLY

These runner/string beans have been grown from beans saved from last year's crop and are more than ready to be moved out from the cosy greenhouse into the earth and sun outside (above left). In Denmark, garden designer Dorthe Kvist successfully grows peaches in her greenhouse (above centre). Alpine strawberries are my favourite fruit to grow (above right) – they need very little tending and each year they produce runners that can be potted up to make new plants.

The saying goes 'nothing tastes as good as home-grown' and in my experience I would have to agree. I love growing our own fruit, vegetables and herbs, and we have dedicated part of the bottom of our garden to edible crops. My husband built two large raised beds in a sunny spot; we currently have strawberries and rhubarb in one, while in the other we rotate what we grow each year (this is good for the soil, and also allows us to experiment with different vegetables – always a learning experience!). We have also planted raspberries, blackberries, blueberries and redcurrants and were lucky that our garden already had established plum, apple and fig trees, all of which crop heavily each year. As well as the delicious fruits, there is the added bonus of beautiful spring blossom displays – we recently planted a cherry tree and I can't wait to see it in blossom for the first time.

If you have the space, growing your own food is a wonderful endeavour, as it is environmentally friendly (cutting down on food miles), inexpensive, really not too difficult and, most importantly, completely tasty. If you only have a small garden, or even if you're restricted to a balcony, try growing some herbs in pots, or even a few strawberries or a tomato plant. You will be surprised at just how much you can grow without needing a full-size garden, and you'll soon find that this becomes an addictive hobby.

MY TOP 10 EASY-TO-GROW VEG

These are my favourites, which I grow year after year.

1. BULB FENNEL

When we moved to our house I sprinkled fennel seeds on a patch of earth, then forgot about them until I noticed a bulb with a hairy stalk appearing. I harvest a few bulbs, save some seeds to add to recipes and leave the rest to fall, and each year more fennel appears.

2. CARROTS

I sprinkle carrot seeds directly into raised beds, covering them lightly with soil. When shoots appear, I thin them out and wait patiently for the crop to grow. They are always fresh and sweet.

3. PEAS

Home-grown peas have a sweet flavour no frozen variety can compete with. The flowers resemble sweet peas without the scent, so they look pretty while growing as well as tasting so good.

4. COURGETTES

One of my earliest memories is helping Grandpa harvest courgettes/zucchini from his veggie patch. The yellow varieties are my favourites as they taste buttery.

5. ONIONS

These will grow in almost any soil and prefer a warm, sunny site.

6. SALAD LEAVES

Crunchy salad leaves are quick and easy to grow from seed. Use the cut-and-come-again method of cutting the outer leaves and leaving the centres to grow for fresh salad all summer long.

7. GARLIC

Best planted in late autumn or early winter. Break up the bulbs and plant individual cloves just below the soil surface 15 cm/6 inches apart and in rows 30 cm/12 inches apart.

8. CUCUMBERS

I admit I cheat and buy a small plant started off in a greenhouse. I plant this directly into the veggie patch and water it every evening. Last year one plant yielded over 20 cucumbers!

9. TOMATOES

Tomatoes are so easy to grow and you don't even need a garden - cherry varieties can be cultivated in a window box while grow bags are perfect for decking or balconies.

10. HERBS

Not strictly vegetables, but these could not be omitted because there are so many unique flavours. Always plant mint in a pot, as it spreads rapidly.

ADDED BENEFITS

Two of the lovely side effects of growing your own are sharing your produce with neighbours and friends, especially if you have a glut, and trying out new recipes to make the most of fresh produce. Grow whichever vegetables suit the conditions of your garden, and don't be afraid to experiment.

MAKE / BOTANICAL COCKTAILS

I love making and drinking botanical cocktails - they look as good as they taste and will be a talking point at any garden gathering. I mix together good-quality gin, elderflower cordial, apple juice and lemonade in a large glass jug, and add lots of ice. For the perfect finishing touch, add fresh thyme and sage leaves and some edible flowers - here I've used lavender heads and cornflowers - and serve in glasses with more ice. I like to use old-fashioned, heavy cut-glass crystal tumblers. For a non-alcoholic version (or for serving to children), simply omit the gin. Always shake the flowers before using, to make sure there aren't any bugs lurking between the petals.

GROWING IN RAISED BEDS

Veggie patches can be both functional and attractive garden features, while raised beds make weeding, sowing and harvesting a lot easier. My husband made our raised beds from scaffolding planks – on the left you can see one filled with chives and salad leaves, with netting at the back for peas and beans to scramble up. First we cleared the ground and dug out all the weed roots, then constructed the two beds, filling them with good-quality soil. A gravel path around each bed makes it easy to garden in all weathers. Each winter we fertilize the beds with manure and homemade compost to enrich the soil. We also grow veg in containers and have discovered that old water tanks (left) make ideal containers because they are deep and look good in the garden. We have also upcycled an old wheelbarrow – here it is filled with potato plants.

PRIZED ALLOTMENTS

I feel a connection to allotments, as my grandpa, his brother (my Great Uncle Harry) and my dad used to share a plot, growing veggies for the family. Here is the most inspiring allotment I've ever seen – Lou's plot 22 (@thelittleredrobin via Instagram). There are peas growing up twiggy supports, cucumbers growing around an old wooden ladder and nasturtiums weaving in and out.

MAKE / STENCILLED PLANT LABELS

Plant labels are essential to help you remember which seeds you have sown. To make these labels you need timber mouldings (I buy these in strips from a DIY store), a saw, a letter stencil and permanent white marker pen. Saw the length of timber into 25-cm/10-inch lengths and cut away two triangles at one end to create a point to push into the earth. Write the plant name on the wood using the letter stencil and the white marker pen.

MAKE / SLATE & WOOD MARKERS

These stylish markers are handmade by Marc Winstanley. Use salvaged or scrap pieces of slate (such as broken roof slates), and pallets are a good source of free or inexpensive wood. Saw the pallet into strips roughly 4 x 35 cm/1½ x 14 inches, cutting a point at one end. Using a tile cutter, cut the slate into pieces roughly 18 x 12 cm/7 x 4½ inches. Drill screw holes in the slate in the middle of the two long sides and grind off any sharp corners. Screw to the non-pointed end of the pallet strip. Use a chalk pen to write on the labels.

D & C

TOP TIP

Decorate the wicker basket on a bike and add a flower-filled box to the luggage rack with monkshood, campanula, dahlias, candytuft, mallow and cosmos.

SOURCES

PLANT AND FLOWER SHOPS AND GARDEN CENTRES TO VISIT

UK

BUCKETS OF BLOOMS
www.bucketsofblooms.co.uk
Flower growers in Hampshire, specializing in seasonal cut flowers for weddings and celebrations. Their beautiful fresh blooms are also sold by the bucketful.

BURFORD GARDEN COMPANY
Shilton Road
Burford
Oxfordshire OX18 4PA
www.burford.co.uk
This stylish garden centre in the heart of the Cotswolds also offers rustic-chic homewares and a gift shop, café and art gallery.

DAVID AUSTIN ROSES
Bowling Green Lane
Albrighton
Wolverhampton WV7 3HB
www.davidaustinroses.com
Breeders of old English roses. Visit their fabulous rose garden in Shropshire.

MOUTAN GARDEN
Newlyns Farm Shop
Lodge Farm
North Warnborough
Hook
Hampshire RG29 1HA
www.moutan.co.uk
Lovely garden gift shop selling plants, flowers, garden furniture and accessories plus gifts and homewares.

PETERSHAM NURSERIES
Church Lane
Off Petersham Road
Richmond
Surrey TW10 7AB
www.petershamnurseries.com
An inspiring shop and nursery selling gorgeous gardenalia and plants plus a teahouse and restaurant, all in a magical setting.

THE ROYAL HORTICULTURAL SOCIETY
www.rhs.org.uk
The RHS owns four major gardens around the UK that can be visited for inspiration. Their famed flower shows include the prestigious Chelsea Flower Show, held every May since 1912.

SARAH RAVEN'S GARDEN AND COOKERY SCHOOL
Perch Hill Farm
Willingford Lane
Brightling
Robertsbridge TN32 5HP
www.sarahraven.com
A wide and wonderful range of seeds, bulbs, plants and gardening kits as well as garden, food and cookery courses. Check the website for open days.

SCARLET & VIOLET
79 Chamberlayne Road
London NW10 3JJ
scarlet-violet.myshopify.com
An inspiring florist offering amazing bouquets made from fresh flowers, and a place full of botanical scents, chatter and creativity.

SWEDEN & DENMARK

BLOMSTERSKURET
www.blomsterskuret.dk
A pretty little flower shed in Copenhagen selling fresh blooms, plants and accessories.

LÖDDEKÖPING PLANKSKOLA
www.plantis.org
A stylish Swedish garden centre with an array of plants, pots and garden decorations in an inspiring setting.

ROSENDALS TRÄDGÅRD
www.rosendalstradgard.se
Rosendals Garden Foundation espouses biodynamic farming practices. They also have a fabulous shop and cafe and offer events and workshops as well as 'pick your own' flowers in the summer months.

ZETAS TRÄDGÅRD
www.zetas.se
I enjoyed visiting Zetas near Stockholm, Sweden. They sell plants, garden furniture and home accessories and their store is styled beautifully.

USA

TERRAIN
www.shopterrain.com
Gorgeous home and garden furniture, containers and plants. They have a few stores in the US and I'm hoping to visit them all, but in the meantime I love following them on Pinterest @terrain.

URBAN GARDEN CENTRE
www.urbangardennyc.com
New York's largest garden centre; a resource for plants, seed, tools and accessories.

GARDENALIA AND OUTDOOR FURNITURE

&HOBBS
www.andhobbs.com
Libby Hobbs, the woman behind this independent store, has a great eye for unusual pieces and celebrates local makers and designers.

THE COUNTRY BROCANTE
Griffin House
West St
Midhurst
West Sussex GU299NQ
www.countrybrocante.co.uk
Vintage items for home and garden. They also host fairs and brocantes, bringing together different dealers.

PACKHOUSE
Hewett's Kilns
Tongham Road
Runfold
Farnham GU10 1PJ
www.packhouse.com
A unique lifestyle store offering an ever-changing array of gardenalia and vintage buys for the garden.

GARDENALIA AND OUTDOOR FURNITURE TO CHECK OUT ONLINE

CROCUS
www.crocus.co.uk
Online garden centre offering a wide variety of furniture, accessories and equipment as well as plants and horticultural supplies.

FERMOB
www.fermob.com
French outdoor furniture manufacturer.

GARDEN TRADING
www.gardentrading.co.uk
Stylish garden accessories, storage, and furniture.

GREIGE
www.greige.co.uk
Garden furniture and decorative accessories, including jute outdoor rugs, lanterns and hammocks.

GRYTHTTAN STÅLMÖBLER
www.grythyttan.net
Swedish garden furniture company offering chic and streamlined designs.

MANUFACTUM
www.manufactum.co.uk
German retailer selling elegant, minimalist home and garden products.

GARDEN ACCESSORIES

ANTHROPOLOGIE
www.anthropologie.com
Unique plant pots, vases and wares for home and garden.

BASIL AND FORD
www.basilandford.com
Neon screen-printed botanical prints and homewares.

BASKET BASKET
www.basketbasket.co.uk
Baskets of all shapes and sizes, all of them eco-friendly, handmade and fairly traded.

BORÅSTAPETER
www.borastapeter.se
Classic, modern and inspiring wallpaper designs since 1905.

BLOOMINGVILLE
www.bloomingville.com
Stylish Nordic home and garden accessories.

FABULOUS VINTAGE FINDS
www.fabulousvintagefinds.co.uk
Zinc containers, stone urns, planters, benches, French café tables and chairs for the garden. Check their website for upcoming fairs and events.

HOUSE DOCTOR
www.housedoctor.dk
Decorative pots and vases.

LITTLE GREENE
www.littlegreene.com
A lovely collection of colours.

NADIN NÖBOM
www.nadianorbom.com
Nadia is an illustrator and florist at Rosendals Trädgård, where she finds inspiration for her pictures and prints.

THE OLD YARD
www.theoldyard.co.uk
Vintage, industrial and bespoke furniture, lighting and decorative items.

PLANKBRIDGE
www.plankbridge.com
Bespoke shepherd huts handmade in Dorset, UK.

TINEKHOME
www.tinekhome.com
Stylish garden furniture and accessories.

GARDEN LIGHTING

LIGHTS4FUN
www.light4fun.co.uk
Fantastic range of outdoor lighting to suit all gardens.

LOVE INC
www.loveincltd.co.uk
LED Neon lighting for both the home and garden.

INSPIRING GARDEN STYLE INSTAGRAMMERS

@krullskrukker
@Meltdesignstudio
@arstidensbasta
@vilasmedsbo
@janecumberbatch
@thelittleredrobin
@gertrudsrum
@lenasskoghem
@vildevioler.dk
@_garaget
@clausdalby
@florista_malmo
@lobsterandswan
@familjengron
@hakesgard
@mariekenolsen
@cathy.pyle
@the_bowerbird
@purplearea1
@gandgorgeousflowers
@shopterrain
@zetastradgard
@lavenderandleeks
@Floramorkrukatos
@petershamnurseries
@cat.persson
@inspirationalordinarydays
@annae1969
@purpleeara1
@foundandfavour
@themontydon
@mhairi-stella

PICTURE CREDITS

All photography by Rachel Whiting except where stated.
Key: ph= photographer, a=above, b=below, r=right, l=left, c=centre.

Endpapers The home and garden of Russ and Louise Grace; 1 The home and garden of Catarina Persson in Sweden; 2–3 The garden of Debbie Smail, West Sussex; 4–6 Styled by Selina Lake at her home; 7ar & bl The garden of Susann Larsson in Lomma, Sweden; 7 br The home and garden of Lena Wallin in Sweden; 8 The home and garden of Russ and Louise Grace; 9 The family home and garden of Clara Sewell-Knight; 10–11 The garden of Anna Malm in Sweden; 12 ac ph. Selina Lake/her own garden; 12 ar The garden of Anna Malm in Sweden; 12 bl ph. Selina Lake/Mant Shop, Copenhagen; 12 br ph. Selina Lake/Blomsterkuret, Copenhagen; 12–13 c Burford Garden Company www.burford.co.uk; 12–13 b The home and garden of Charlotta Jörgensen in Lomma, Sweden; 13 al Styled by Selina Lake at her home; 13 ar ph. Sussie Bell/National Garden Scheme – The Old Rectory, Farnborough www.ngs.org.uk; 13 ac The home and garden of Catarina Persson in Sweden; 13 c ph. Courtesy of Green & Gorgeous Flower Farm; 13 b Mhairi-Stella Illustration www.mhairi-stella.com; 13 br Styled by Selina Lake at her home; 14 Photo courtesy of Mayfield Lavender Ltd www.mayfieldlavender.com; 15 ph. Debi Treloar/David Austin Roses www.davidaustinroses.co.uk; 16 l ph. Courtesy of Danish Horticultural Society/'Wild and wonderful urban oasis' designed by Dorthe Kvist, meltdesignstudio.com; 16 r ph. Heather Edwards/GAP photos–Garden Design: James Callicott; 17 Eriksdal Lunden Allotment Gardens www.eriksdalslunden.se; 18 Stiftelsen Rosendals Trädgård www.rosendalstradgard.se; 19 ph. Courtesy of Green & Gorgeous Flower Farm; 20 al ph. www.marimoimages.co.uk /Petersham Nurseries Café; 20 bl Burford Garden Company www.burford.co.uk; 20 ar ph. Stephanie Wolff Photography www.stephaniewolff.co.uk/Petersham Nurseries; 20 br & 21 Zetas Trädgård www.zetas.se; 22 l ph. Hallam Creations/Shutterstock.com; 22 r ph. Anton U/Shutterstock.com; 23 al ph. Polly Wreford; 23 ar The home and garden of Russ and Louise Grace; 23 br ph. Tatiana Makotra/Shutterstock.com; 24 al ph. E Kramar/Shutterstock.com; 24 ar ph. Ioana Rut/Shutterstock.com; 24 bl ph. Predrag Lukic/Shutterstock.com; 25 al Styled by Selina Lake at her home; 25 ar ph. Kim Lightbody; 26–27 Stiftelsen Rosendals Trädgård www.rosendalstradgard.se; 28 ar Stiftelsen Rosendals Trädgård www.rosendalstradgard.se; 28 bl The home and garden of Charlotta Jörgensen in Lomma, Sweden; 29 The garden of Debbie Smail, West Sussex; 30 b The London home of the interiors blogger Katy Orme (apartmentapothecary.com); 31 The home and garden of Lena Wallin in Sweden; 34 Dorthe Kvist garden designer, author and blogger; 35 al & ac The home and garden of Catarina Persson in Sweden; 35 ar The home and garden of Charlotta Jörgensen in Lomma, Sweden; 36–37 Styled by Selina Lake at her home; 38 & 39 al The garden of Anna Malm in Sweden; 39 ar Styled by Selina Lake at her home; 39 bl The home and garden of Catarina Persson in Sweden; 40 l & r The home and garden of Lena Wallin in Sweden; 40 c & 41 The home and garden of Catarina Persson in Sweden; 42 Styled by Selina Lake at her home; 43 al The home and garden of Lena Wallin in Sweden; 43 br Stiftelsen Rosendals Trädgård www.rosendalstradgard.se; 44 The garden of Debbie Smail, West Sussex; 45 Dorthe Kvist garden designer, author and blogger; 46 The garden of Debbie Smail, West Sussex; 47 Styled by Selina Lake at her home; 48 l The home and garden of Catarina Persson in Sweden; 48 r The garden of Debbie Smail, West Sussex; 49 l Styled by Selina Lake at her home; 50 l The garden of Anna Malm in Sweden; 50 r The home and garden of Lena Wallin in Sweden; 51 The garden of Debbie Smail, West Sussex; 54 The family home and garden of Clara Sewell-Knight; 55 The garden of Susann Larsson in Lomma, Sweden; 56–57 Styled by Selina Lake at her home; 57 r The home and garden of Charlotta Jörgensen in Lomma, Sweden; 58 Styled by Selina Lake at her home; 59 The garden of Susann Larsson in Lomma, Sweden; 60 l The garden of Debbie Smail, West Sussex; 60 r Dorthe Kvist garden designer, author and blogger; 61 al The family home and garden of Clara Sewell-Knight; 61 ar & bl The home and garden of Russ and Louise Grace; 61 br The family home and garden of Clara Sewell-Knight; 62 al The family home and garden of Clara Sewell-Knight; 62 ar The garden of Debbie Smail, West Sussex; 62 br The home and garden of Russ and Louise Grace; 63 l The garden of Anna Malm in Sweden; 63 r The home and garden of Lena Wallin in Sweden; 64 al ph. Debi Treloar; 68–69 Stiftelsen Rosendals Trädgård www.rosendalstradgard.se; 70 al Styled by Selina Lake at her home; 70 ar Stiftelsen Rosendals Trädgård www.rosendalstradgard.se; 70 bl The home and garden of Charlotta Jörgensen in Lomma, Sweden; 70 br & 71 Styled by Selina Lake at her home; 74 Styled by Selina Lake at her home; 76 al Styled by Selina Lake at her home; 76 ar The garden of Debbie Smail, West Sussex; 77 al Dorthe Kvist garden designer, author and blogger; 77 ar The home and garden of Charlotta Jörgensen in Lomma, Sweden; 78 Styled by Selina Lake at her home; 80 al & ar The home and garden of Russ and Louise Grace; 80 b Dorthe Kvist garden designer, author and blogger; 81 The home and garden of Russ and Louise Grace; 82 The garden of Debbie Smail, West Sussex; 83 l The home and garden of Russ and Louise Grace; 83 r The garden of Debbie Smail, West Sussex; 84–85 Stiftelsen Rosendals Trädgård www.rosendalstradgard.se; 88–89 The home and garden of Charlotta Jörgensen in Lomma, Sweden; 92 The summerhouse of photographer Cathy Pyle www.cathypyle.com; 93 l Styled by Selina Lake at her home; 93 r The summerhouse of photographer Cathy Pyle www.cathypyle.com; 94–96 The home and garden of Lena Wallin in Sweden; 97 l & 97 ar Dorthe Kvist garden designer, author and blogger; 97 br Styled by Selina Lake at her home; 98–99 Stiftelsen Rosendals Trädgård www.rosendalstradgard.se; 100 The garden of Susann Larsson in Lomma, Sweden; 101 l The family home and garden of Clara Sewell-Knight; 101 c Eriksdal Lunden Allotment Gardens www.eriksdalslunden.se; 101 r The garden of Susann Larsson in Lomma, Sweden; 104 al Styled by Selina Lake at her home; 104 br The garden of Anna Malm in Sweden; 105 Styled by Selina Lake at her home; 106 a, bl & bc The garden of Anna Malm in Sweden; 107–109 The garden of Debbie Smail, West Sussex; 110–111 The garden of Anna Malm in Sweden; 112–113 Styled by Selina Lake at her home; 114–115 l Dorthe Kvist garden designer, author and blogger; 115 r The home and garden of Lena Wallin in Sweden; 116–117 The home and garden of Catarina Persson in Sweden; 118–119 Mhairi-Stella Illustration www.mhairi-stella.com; 120 The garden of Susann Larsson in Lomma, Sweden; 121 The home and garden of Catarina Persson in Sweden; 122 l Dorthe Kvist garden designer, author and blogger; 122 r & 123 The garden of Susann Larsson in Lomma, Sweden; 124 Dorthe Kvist garden designer, author and blogger; 125 l Stiftelsen Rosendals Trädgård www.rosendalstradgard.se; 126 Dorthe Kvist garden designer, author and blogger; 127 The home and garden of Lena Wallin in Sweden; 128 al & ac The garden of Anna Malm in Sweden; 128 ar & 129 The home and garden of Catarina Persson in Sweden; 130–131 Styled by Selina Lake at her home; 134–135 Styled by Selina Lake at her home; 136–138 Dorthe Kvist garden designer, author and blogger; 139 al & br Dorthe Kvist garden designer, author and blogger; 139 ar ph. Selina Lake/her own garden; 140–141 Stiftelsen Rosendals Trädgård www.rosendalstradgard.se; 142–143 The garden of Anna Malm in Sweden; 144 The home and garden of Charlotta Jörgensen in Lomma, Sweden; 145 l Styled by Selina Lake at her home; 145 c Dorthe Kvist garden designer, author and blogger; 145 r ph. Tara Fisher; 146 ph. Tara Fisher; 147 ph. Emma Mitchell; 148 l & br The home and garden of Russ and Louise Grace; 148 ar ph. Tara Fisher; 149 al The home and garden of Lena Wallin in Sweden; 149 ar Styled by Selina Lake at her home; 149 b The garden of Debbie Smail, West Sussex; 150–153 The home and garden of Russ and Louise Grace; 155 The home and garden of Charlotta Jörgensen in Lomma, Sweden; 157 Stiftelsen Rosendals Trädgård www.rosendalstradgard.se; 160 Stiftelsen Rosendals Trädgård www.rosendalstradgard.se.

BUSINESS CREDITS

SELINA LAKE
Author and stylist
www.selinalake.co.uk
IG and Pinterest: @selinalake
Pages 4–6, 12 ac, 12 bl, 12 br, 13 al, 13 br, 25 al, 36, 37, 39 ar, 42, 47, 49 l, 56, 57, 58, 70 al, 70 br, 71, 74, 76 al, 78, 93 l, 97 br, 104 al, 105, 112–113, 130, 131, 134, 135, 139 ar, 145 l, 149 ar.

ERIKSDAL LUNDEN ALLOTMENT GARDENS
www.eriksdalslunden.se
Pages 17, 101 c.

RUSS & LOUISE GRACE
The Little Red Robin
Artisan garden frames, plant supports and flowers
www.thelittleredrobin.com
E: info@thelittleredrobin.com
Endpapers, pages 8, 23 ar, 61 ar, 61 bl, 62 br, 80 al, 80 ar, 81, 83 l, 148 l, 148 br, 150–153.

CHARLOTTA JÖRGENSEN
IG: @inspirationordinarydays
www.bo-laget.se
Pages 12, 13 b, 28 bl, 35 ar, 57 r, 70 bl, 77 ar, 88, 89, 121, 144, 155.

DORTHE KVIST
Garden designer, author and blogger
Designer/Founder
MELTdesignstudio
T: +45 2615 2906
E: dk@meltdesignstudio.com
www.meltdesignstudio.com
IG: @meltdesignstudio
Pages 34, 45, 60 r, 77 al, 80 b, 97 l, 97 ar, 114, 115 l, 122 l, 124, 126, 136–138, 139 al, 139 br, 145 c.

SUSANN LARSSON
IG: @purplearea1
E: susann@purplearea1.com
www.purplearea.se
Pages 7 ar, 7 bl, 55, 59, 100, 101 r, 120, 122 r, 123.

ANNA MALM
IG: @Annae1969
Pages 10–11, 12 ar, 38, 39 al, 50 l, 63 l, 104 br, 106 a, 106 bl, 106 bc, 110–111, 128 al, 128 ac, 142, 143.

MHAIRI-STELLA ILLUSTRATION
www.mhairi-stella.com
Pages 13 b, 118, 119.

CATARINA PERSSON
IG: @cat.persson
Facebook: trädgårdsfröjd
Pages 1, 13 ac, 35 al, 35 ac, 39 bl, 40 c, 41, 48 l, 116, 117, 128 ar, 129.

CATHY PYLE PHOTOGRAPHER
www.cathypyle.com
Pages 92, 93 r.

CLARA SEWELL-KNIGHT
IG: @foundandfavour
Pages 9, 54, 61 al, 61 ar, 61 bl, 61 br, 62 al, 101 l.

DEBBIE SMAIL
IG: @the_bowerbird
Pages 2–3, 29, 44, 46, 48 r, 51, 60 l, 6 ar, 76 ar, 82, 83 r, 107–109, 149 b.

STIFTELSEN ROSENDALS TRÄDGÅRD
Rosendalsterrassen 12
115 21 Stockholm
Tel. 08 545 812 70
info@rosendalstradgard.se
www.rosendalstradgard.se
Pages 18, 26, 27, 28 ar, 43 br, 68, 69, 70 ar, 84, 85, 98, 99, 125 l, 140–141, 157, 160.

LENA WALLIN
IG: @lenasskoghem
Pages 7 br, 31, 40 l, 40 r, 43 al, 50 r, 63 r, 94–96, 115 r, 127, 149 al.

ZETAS TRÄDGÅRD
www.zetas.se
Pages 20 br, 21.

INDEX

Page numbers in italic refer to the illustrations

ACKNOWLEDGMENTS

Garden Style is my eighth book, and I'm thrilled with the result. A huge thank you to all the team at RPS for making it come to life. Producing *Garden Style* has been a joy from start to finish and I have relished using my styling skills to create garden displays and outdoor rooms in lovely locations. Rachel Whiting, you have captured the essence of *Garden Style* so beautifully with your photography and it's been lovely working with you again – I had so much fun on our travels. Thank you for the gorgeous images and fond memories of a glorious summer.

Perhaps the best thing about working on this book has been visiting wonderful gardens and, along the way, meeting so many inspirational and generous gardeners. A huge thank you to the garden owners – I have been truly inspired by you all. Thanks too for the gardening tips, plant cuttings and delicious lunches made from home-grown produce.

I would also like to thank all the fabulous shops, garden centres and companies who supplied many of the props, plants and furniture featured in the book. Big thanks to those who support my work and projects via social media. I really appreciate your lovely comments, likes and book love and I'd love to see your own *Garden Style* pics – please tag me via social media @selinalake #gardenstyle

Last, but not least, I'd like to thank my parents for their continued support (and for keeping our garden in check while we are away). Thanks also go to my Nanna, Doreen Howard-Baylis, for providing me with garden inspiration from a young age, to my friend Sussie Bell, for all the plants and advice, and to my amazing husband, Dave, who made our outdoor space into a garden – working with you on our garden is the best. Love you x